Helping Hands

Small Motor Skills Projects and Activities

Written by Denise Bieniek

Illustrated by Paige Billin-Frye

10 9 8 7 6 5 4 3

Troll Early Learning Activities

Troll Early Learning Activities is a classroom-tested series designed to provide time-pressured teachers with a wide range of theme-related projects and activities to enhance lesson plans and enrich the curriculum. Each book focuses on a different area of early childhood learning, from math and writing to art and science. Using a wide range of activities, each title in this series is chockful of innovative ideas, handy reproducible pages, puzzles and games, classroom projects, suggestions for bulletin boards and learning centers, and much more.

With highly interactive student projects and teacher suggestions that make learning fun, Troll Early Learning Activities is an invaluable classroom resource you'll turn to again and again. We hope you will enjoy using the worksheets and activities presented in these books. And we know your students will benefit from the dynamic, creative learning environment you have created!

Titles in this series:

Metric Conversion Chart

1 inch = 2.54 cm	1 foot = .305 m	1 yard = .914 m
1 mile = 1.61 km	1 fluid ounce = 29.573 ml	1 cup = .24 l
1 pint = .473 l	1 teaspoon = 4.93 ml	1 tablespoon = 14.78 ml

Five Little Monkeys Fingerplay

Materials:

- crayons
- scissors
- 1" x 3" strips of construction paper
- transparent tape
- glue

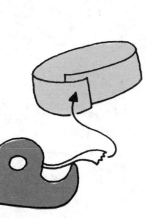

Directions:

1. Reproduce the monkey and crocodile patterns on page 6 as many times as necessary to make a set of five monkeys and one crocodile for each student. Have the children color the figures and cut them out.

2. Demonstrate how to make a ring with a strip of 1" x 3" construction paper by overlapping the ends and taping them closed. Instruct each student to make six rings.

3. Have students glue one monkey to the front of each of their first five rings and then glue the crocodile to the front of their sixth rings. Have each student place the five monkeys on the fingers of one hand and the crocodile on a finger from the other hand.

Five Little Monkeys Sitting in a Tree

Five little monkeys sitting in a tree,
    (*wiggle five fingers with monkey rings on them*)
Just teasing Mr. Crocodile,
    (*wiggle finger with crocodile on it*)
"You can't catch me!"
    (*face monkeys toward crocodile, say in a teasing voice*)
Along comes Mr. Crocodile,
    (*crocodile moves slowly toward monkeys*)
Just as quiet as can be,
"Snap!"
    (*hand with crocodile ring grabs one monkey and places it on floor*)

Four little monkeys sitting in a tree . . .

4. When everybody has their animal rings on, teach the class the poem above about five monkeys who liked to tease.

5. Continue the poem until there are no monkeys left sitting in the tree. Encourage students to be as silly as they can when teasing Mr. Crocodile. They may wish to make faces and teasing noises as they chant "You can't catch me!"

6. Ask students to count the number of monkeys still sitting in the tree before beginning the next verse. Then help them make up subtraction equations. For example, one might say, "Five monkeys take away one monkey leaves four monkeys," or "Five minus one equals four."

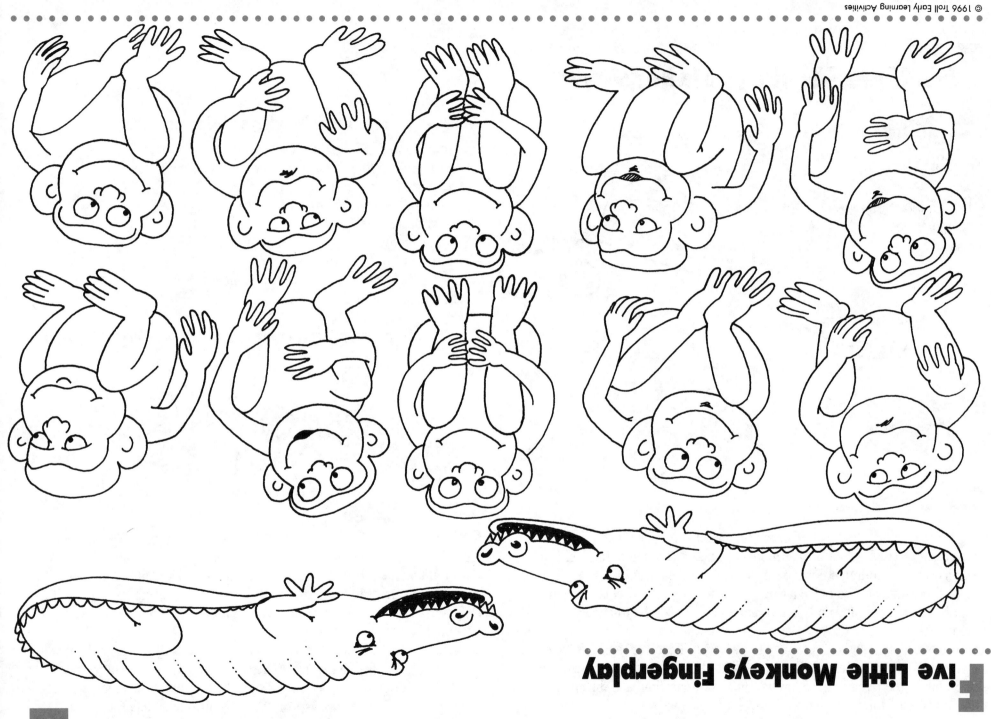

Five Little Monkeys Fingerplay

"This Little Piggy" Cake

Materials:

- 1/2 cup butter or margarine
- 1 cup sugar
- 2 eggs
- 3/4 teaspoon vanilla
- 2 cups sifted flour
- 2 teaspoons baking powder
- 1/4 teaspoon salt
- 2/3 cup milk
- mixing bowls

- rotary beaters
- measuring spoons
- 2 round 8" cake pans
- cookie sheet
- vanilla frosting
- red food coloring
- plastic knives
- small candies
- plates and forks

Directions:

1. Lea... cup of butter, 2 eggs, ...f milk out for abou... ...eginning the...

2. ...

4. Add 3/4 teaspoon of vanilla. Ask other volunteers to take turns working the rotary beater. Have other students begin adding 2 cups of flour, 2 teaspoons of baking powder, and 1/4 teaspoon of salt alternately with the 2/3 cup of milk.

5. Grease two round 8" baking pans and pour the batter into them in equal amounts. Bake at 375°F for 25 to 30 minutes.

6. Let cakes cool in pan before frosting. Remove the cakes from the pans and place one on a cookie sheet.

7. Tint a can of vanilla frosting with red food coloring to make pink frosting. Frost one cake with the pink frosting. Cut ears, a snout, and a bow tie for the pig from the other cake, as shown.

8. Place these parts in position on and around the pig face, and frost. Use small candies to make eyes, nose holes, a mouth, and decorations on the bow tie. Cut, serve, and enjoy!

Materials:

- scissors
- differe...

- different-colored flannel pieces
- safety pins
- hole puncher
- yarn or embroidery thread
- large-eyed blunt needles
- batting or stuffing
- glue
- collage materials

2.

3.

4.

6.

7.

8.

9.

Directions:

1. Ask each student to choose one of the patterns on pages 9 and 10 for a sewing project. Reproduce the selected figure once for each child.

2. Have children cut out the figures.

3. Cut flannel pieces slightly larger than the patterns. Help each student pin his or her pattern onto two pieces of flannel and cut the flannel to the pattern shape. For the duck feet, have students cut one each and put aside.

4. Remove the paper patterns from the flannel cutouts. Help students punch holes around the edges of the patterns, about 1" apart.

5. Demonstrate how to thread a needle with yarn or embroidery thread. You will have to pinch the ends of the yarn before threading the needle, since the yarn untwists easily. Cut an approximate 1' length of yarn or thread for each student and have students thread their needles.

6. Have children knot the free end of the yarn through one of the holes along the flannel pattern edges. Then show students how to bring the needle through the hole next to the knotted one from the back. Be sure to remind them to pull the yarn taut before inserting the needle through the next hole, this time from front to back.

7. Have each student continue sewing his or her animal pattern until there is 4" left open. Demonstrate how to stuff the animal with stuffing, a small bit at a time, until it is full. Continue sewing until the last hole.

8. Cut off the yarn, leaving about 3" excess. Knot this end through the last hole.

9. Students may use collage materials or flannel scraps to add eyes and other features. To complete the duck, glue the feet to the base of the body. Flannel scraps will also be useful for making clothes for the doll.

Dot-to-Dot Sewing

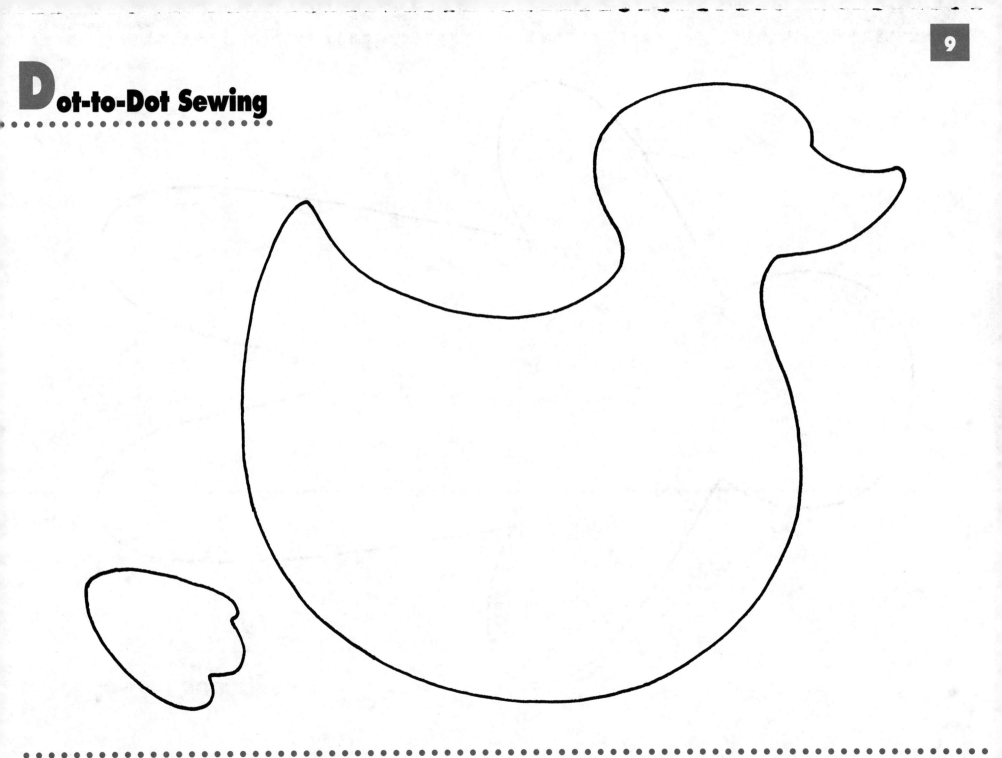

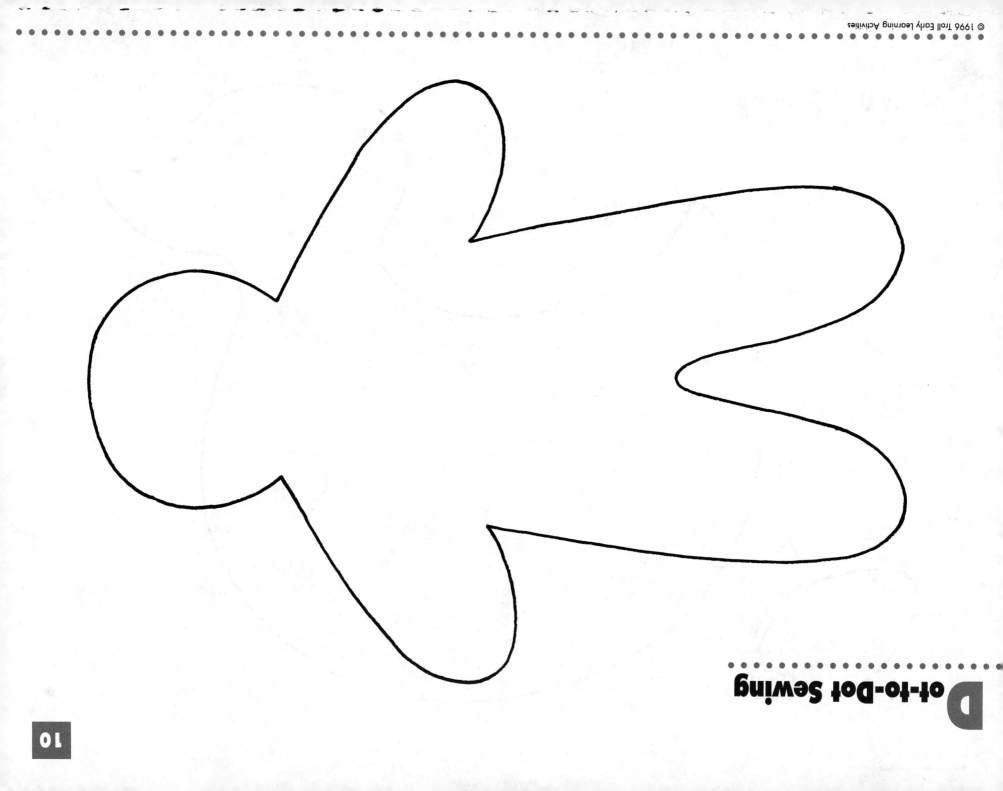

Hidden Letters

Begin at the first alphabetical letter in each group. Then connect the dots by following the letters in alphabetical order. On the lines provided, write a word that begins with the letter you formed.

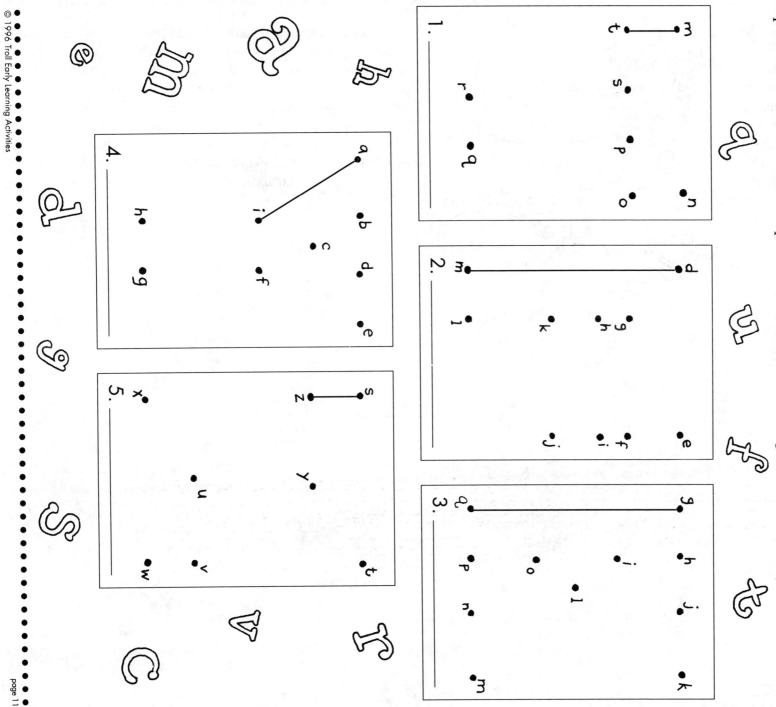

© 1996 Troll Early Learning Activities

Dough Doodles

Materials:

- flour
- salt
- water
- food coloring
- mixing bowl
- mixing spoon
- resealable container

Directions:

1. Mix two parts flour with one part salt. To make colored dough, squeeze ten drops of food coloring into a cup of water. Add water slowly to the mixture, stirring as you proceed.

2. Continue adding water until the dough becomes too difficult to stir. Then use hands to knead the dough. If the dough is too sticky, add more flour; if it is too dry, add a bit more water.

3. Begin students' experiences modeling dough using the dough alone. Each child should receive an amount at least as big as your fist. See how many techniques students can think of for making shapes and designs.

4. Discuss the texture of the dough when it is newly made and when it has dried out a bit. Which is easier to mold? Mix batches of dough in different colors. Does combining dough of different colors make new colors?

5. Some great materials to use with the dough are: craft sticks, cookie cutters, a garlic press, an egg slicer, rolling pins, and anything having a distinctive design, such as a ring or a fork.

6. Students may make designs on flattened dough and play guessing games with their friends, such as asking who can name the object or objects used to make the design. The children may also recreate their designs on paper when finished and create a dough design book. The book may be used by other students who want to copy the designs, or it may act as a springboard for other design ideas.

7. Dough is also a good source of imaginative play in learning centers, such as the block area and dramatic play center. Dough can become a person, a car, an animal, a food, a baby's bottle, or a stylish piece of jewelry.

Creative Collages

1. Ask students to become collectors. Tell the children to try to collect various kinds of things that others no longer need or want, such as scraps of wrapping paper, ribbons, cookie cutters, boxes, fabric, wood, cushions, Styrofoam packing, baby clothes, jar lids, buttons, keys, or anything else that might be transformed into something useful. Encourage the class to bring in the items they've collected to use in various class projects.

2. Collage is a great way to bring together all the different bits and pieces left over from other projects. Collage may also be used to introduce new materials and allow students to get a hands-on feel for them.

3. Students may wish to create their own methods for attaching items to their collages. For those who have a problem deciding, demonstrate how to place a glue layer down first wherever they wish a material to go and then place the material on the glue. Or show students how to apply glue to the back of a material and gently press it to a surface. Sometimes putting glue into a cup and using a cotton swab to brush it onto smaller materials helps conserve glue as well as make cleanup a lot easier.

4. Themes are good for giving focus to collages. Holiday themes lend themselves well to collage. Certain colors of materials bring to mind various holidays; for example, orange and brown are usually associated with fall and Halloween. A birthday collage could have pictures from magazines of cakes, bits of ribbon and wrapping paper, a candle, and the age of the student made from yarn or fabric. Other themes might include shapes, colors, numbers, texture, length, letters, the home, friends and family, and seasons.

5. Collage may also be used as a quiet art activity for a group of students during free time. Make sure students have plenty of glue, materials, scissors, and different types of paper in an art center. Collages may be done on paper, trays, or large sheets of butcher paper. Ask students if they wish to talk about their work and where it might be displayed in the room. If possible, allow students to hang their own work.

Paper Bag Vests

Materials:

- large brown paper grocery bags
- scissors
- crayons or markers
- paints and brushes
- collage materials
- glue
- masking tape
- 3/4" buttons
- thread and needles

Directions:

1. Distribute one large brown paper bag to each student. Show the children how to cut an opening in the middle of one of the larger sides, cutting from the open end to the bottom of the bag.

2. Next, demonstrate how to cut a circle from the bottom of the bag, beginning and ending at the side cut.

3. Demonstrate how to make armholes, by cutting a square from each of the smaller sides where they meet the base of the bag. Help students mark off a square with a dark crayon, about 5" from the base of the bag, and as wide as the bag, on both sides. Ask students to cut along the squares marked on either side of their bags.

4. Ask students to try their vests on. If a vest is too small, cut up the middle of the smaller sides and tape a panel cut from another paper bag in the space.

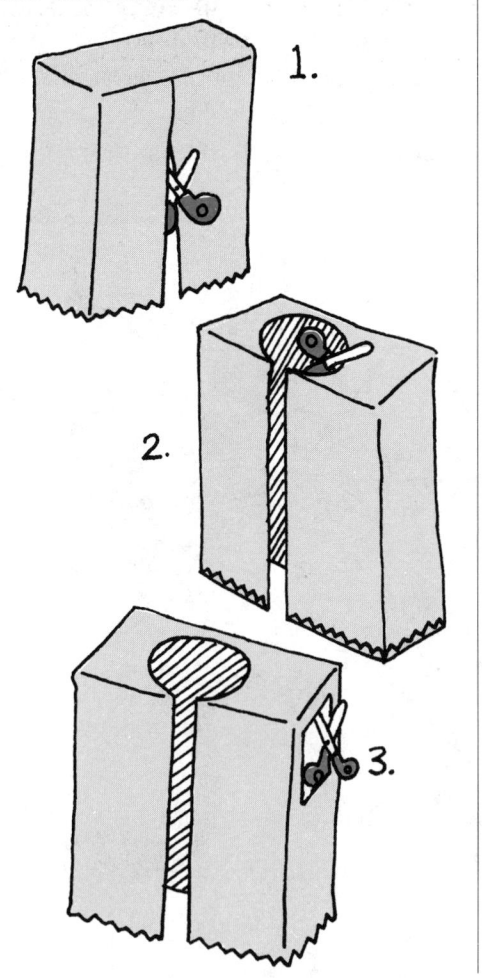

5. Invite students to decorate their vests any way they wish. They may paint designs on them or glue materials to them. Or students may wish to write phrases or popular names (sports figures, musical artists, book or movie characters) across the vests.

6. When the vests have been decorated, show students how to cut buttonholes down the right side of the front of the vests. First, have them mark off the spaces for the holes by measuring down 4" from the collar of the vest, drawing a horizontal line about 1" long and in about 1" from the edge of the vest. Continue measuring and marking down the length of the bag.

7. Ask students to cut pieces of masking tape that are 4" long, one for each buttonhole. Show them how to place the tape pieces over the markings so the tape covers the markings and wraps around to the inside of the vest, underneath the markings. They can then use scissors to slit the hole open.

8. Overlap the buttonhole side of the vest with the other side. Use a crayon to mark the spots under the buttonholes where the buttons will be added. Use thread and needles to attach buttons. The buttons should be 3/4" in size so they will fit in the holes easily.

9. Have students wear their vests and attempt to button them. Create a chart entitled, "I can button!" When a student completes buttoning his or her vest, ask the student to write his or her name on the chart. Give a round of applause when someone's name is written on the chart. Encourage the class to take their vests home and display their buttoning ability to their families.

Sorting Ideas

1. Sorting activities require a great many objects to sort. Again, you may wish to ask students to help collect different objects. Collect enough materials for at least one sorting activity. Buttons, keys, jar lids, lengths of ribbon or string, and bows are excellent things to sort. Many foods also lend themselves to sorting, such as beans, colored candies, pasta, cereals, and apples.

2. For beginning experiences with sorting, distribute materials with obvious differences. Also, begin with simple groupings, such as size, shape, and color. As students become better at discriminating among materials, increase the difficulty of the groupings. When students feel comfortable sorting,

encourage them to create their own object categories.

3. Sorting may be done in muffin tins, circles shaped from yarn, egg cartons, cookie sheets, paper plates, cups, or anything that might hold many small objects. Students may also sort by putting objects into category piles on a table or other flat surface.

4. Sorting becomes more exciting when it is done as part of a race. Students in groups may sort objects by color; the first team to finish sorting their objects is the winner. Other ideas for sorting races are to see which team can make the most categories or the fewest categories.

Finger Painting Fun

1. For basic finger painting fun, cover the floor under the work surface with newspaper. Ask students which colors they would like to use for their paintings. Pour a small amount of each color requested onto the table.

2. Encourage students to use their hands to mix the colors. Ask them to identify the colors they mixed and the new colors they formed.

3. Encourage them to use different parts of their hands to make new designs in the paint. For example, fingernails make narrow lines. The palm of a hand can make an interesting trail. Using just fingertips can lead to fingerprint pictures of animals, people, trees, buildings, and so on.

4. To save a final work of art, lay a piece of paper over the paint and gently press down. Lift the paper at one end and pull up until the opposite end is free of the paint. Or have students paint directly onto finger paint paper.

5. When the children are finished with their paintings, make a wreath of finger-painted hands. Ask the children to press their hands onto a piece of construction paper. When the handprints are dry, have volunteers cut them out.

6. Lay the hand cutouts overlapping in a circle, and glue them together. Decorate with a bow at the top and hang in the room for all to see.

Finger Paint Recipe

1 1/3 cups elastic dry starch
2 cups cold water
6 cups boiling water
2 cups laundry soap, such as Ivory Snow
oil of cloves (1/4 teaspoon)
vegetable coloring

1. Dissolve 1 1/3 cups elastic dry starch into 2 cups of cold water. Stir until smooth.

2. Add 6 cups of boiling water, making sure to stir constantly until the mixture has thickened. (Do not boil for longer than one minute.)

3. Stir in the Ivory Snow and approximately 1/4 teaspoon of oil of cloves. Add vegetable coloring as desired to make different colors of paint.

Fruit and Cheese Kabobs

Materials:

- various fruits
- various cheeses
- plastic knives
- paper plates
- skewers

KABOB COMBINATIONS

Directions:

1. Ask each student to donate a fruit or some cheese. Fruits that work well are grapes, apples, melons, berries, cherries, and bananas. Cheeses that come in blocks work best.

2. Observe the fruits and cheeses with the class. Talk about textures, colors, shapes, and smells. Ask volunteers to cut up the fruits and cheeses into 1" squares. Lay each different fruit and cheese on a different paper plate.

3. Lay skewers down next to the plates. Caution students about the sharpness of the skewer and tell them to be very careful as they load their fruits and cheeses onto the skewers. Invite students to come to the table, take a skewer, hold it by the blunt end, and carefully add their chosen foods to it.

4. Discuss the combinations of food on the skewers before students eat them. Write down all the combinations and see if students can come up with any more while they are enjoying their kabobs. As a follow-up, students may continue creating fruit and cheese kabob combinations not already mentioned.

Great Games

Hot Potato

1. To play "Hot Potato," have students stand or sit in a circle. Pick one student to hold the "potato." The potato may be a real one, or a sock stuffed with fiberfill, or a paper bag stuffed with crumpled newspaper.
2. On the word "Go," tell the first player to pass the potato to the player on his or her right. The potato continues around the circle in this manner. Begin the game slowly and gradually increase the pace of the passing; music is helpful for this purpose.

3. If a player drops the potato, he or she is out and may watch the game from the sidelines. The last player who has not dropped the potato is the winner.
4. Or start a game while playing a lively song. Tell students that when the music stops, the player holding the potato is out of the game. Continue playing until there is only one player left.

Time Bomb

1. To play this game, you will first need a "bomb." To make the bomb, wrap a timer in a sock and pack it in with fiberfill. Close off the opening with a rubber band.
2. Ask students to sit or stand in a circle. Set the "bomb" to go off in three minutes, then hand it to a student. He or she will immediately pass it to the player on the right. Play continues around the circle in this manner.
3. The player holding the bomb when it goes off is out. Continue playing until one player is left.

Hide the Bone

1. Ask students to stand in a line, shoulder to shoulder. Choose one player to be the "dog." The "dog" should stand with his or her back to the others. Give the "bone," a block or other small object, to a player on one end of the line.
2. When the dog says "Woof," have the first player pass the bone to the next player and so on down the line, taking care to conceal the bone from the dog. If the bone gets to the player at the end of the line, he or she should pass it back to the previous player and so on back to the first player again.
3. The dog may say "Woof" again at any time. Whoever has the bone must hold on to it. The dog can then call out the name of the player he or she thinks is holding the bone. If the dog is incorrect, the game begins again with another "Woof." If the dog is correct, the player with the bone becomes the dog.

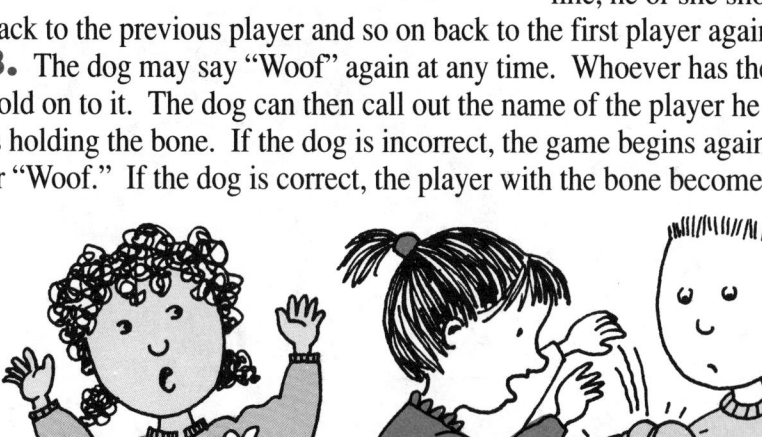

Spoon Relay Races

1. Divide the class into groups of five. Have the groups stand at one end of the room or the gym. Mark off a finish line at the opposite end of the room.

2. Give the first player on each team a large spoon and a hard-boiled egg. Tell the first set of players to go as quickly as possible to the opposite side of the room, cross over the finish line, and then turn around and come back, all without dropping the egg. Each player should then pass the spoon and egg to the next player on his or her team.

3. If an egg falls off a spoon, the player holding it must go back to the starting line and begin again. The first team to complete the task wins.

4. This relay race may also be played with water. Give each team a cup of water. Place an empty cup at the finish line and mark the cup with a piece of colored tape halfway up. Players take a spoonful of water, run to their cups, empty their spoonful of water into the cups, then run back and hand the spoon to the next player. The first team to fill their cup to the tape mark is the winner. Players will probably need to take several turns before their cups are full. This game can get slippery, so caution students to be careful when running!

5. For variety, you may wish to substitute table tennis balls, Styrofoam packing peanuts, small fake fruit from the housekeeping area, or other small and light objects in a spoon relay race.

Snake Hopscotch

1. Play this variation on the game of "Hopscotch." Draw a hopscotch playing field on an outdoor playing surface, as shown.

2. Two to four players may play at a time. Give each player a different stone to use.

3. The first player tosses his or her stone onto the playing field. Players must hop on one foot through each square without touching any lines. If a player touches any lines or places both feet in a square, he or she must return to the start and wait for another turn.

4. When a player gets to the square in which his or her stone has been tossed, he or she must pick up the stone, then hop entirely over that square.

5. When a player reaches the end, he or she must jump on the snake's head with both feet, then jump once more to turn around. Players then proceed back, hopping on one foot as before.

Dress-Up Game

Directions:

1. Ask volunteers to bring in old clothes from older siblings or parents. Make sure the clothes are big enough to fit over students' regular clothing.
2. Divide the class into teams of four students each. Put together an outfit for each line. An outfit may consist of a button-down shirt, a pair of shorts, a jacket, and a pair of shoes. Try to make each outfit have a similar number of buttons, snaps, ties, etc.
3. Have each team line up at one end of an open area. Place an outfit for each team on a chair approximately 15' away.
4. Tell the first player on each team to run to the chair. That player should then put on the outfit, and race back to his or her team.
5. Have the first player tag the hand of the second player in line, then remove the outfit as quickly as possible. The second player then puts the outfit on, and the first player goes to the back of the line.
6. The second player must then run down to the chair, take the outfit off, and return to the line.
7. Play continues until each member of the team has had a turn. The first team to complete all their turns is the winner.

Straw Mazes

Materials:

- 10" x 10" pieces of corrugated cardboard
- straws
- scissors
- glue
- markers
- marbles

Directions:

1. Give pairs of students a piece of corrugated cardboard. Inform them that they will be making mazes and that the cardboard will be the base for their mazes. Ask each pair to lightly sketch out a maze on their base using pencils.

2. When the maze has been approved (there should be a definite entrance and exit), student pairs may begin cutting straws to match the lengths of passages on their mazes. When enough straws have been cut, students may glue them in place on the bases, leaving enough room between them for a marble to pass through.

3. Encourage students to decorate their mazes with markers along the passageways.

4. Ask students to exchange their mazes with other pairs of students. Give the pairs plenty of time to work out the mazes both together and separately. Encourage students to try other mazes and decide which were difficult to do and which were easy to do. They may also wish to criticize classmates' work *constructively* to help them create more challenging mazes. Display the mazes for others to use and enjoy.

Name _____

Amazing Mazemaker
· ·

The Amazing Mazemaker has done it again! See if you can figure out how to get through the castle maze.

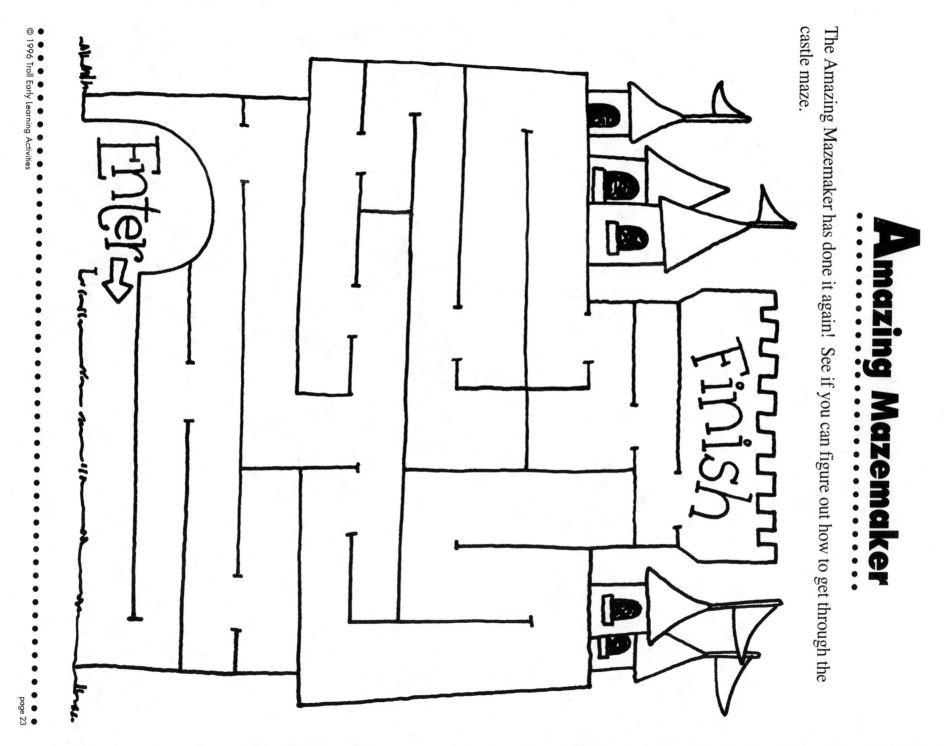

© 1996 Troll Early Learning Activities

Name _____

Crazy Curves

The Amazing Mazemaker has thought of a new way to make mazes. See if you can figure out how to wind your way through this tricky maze.

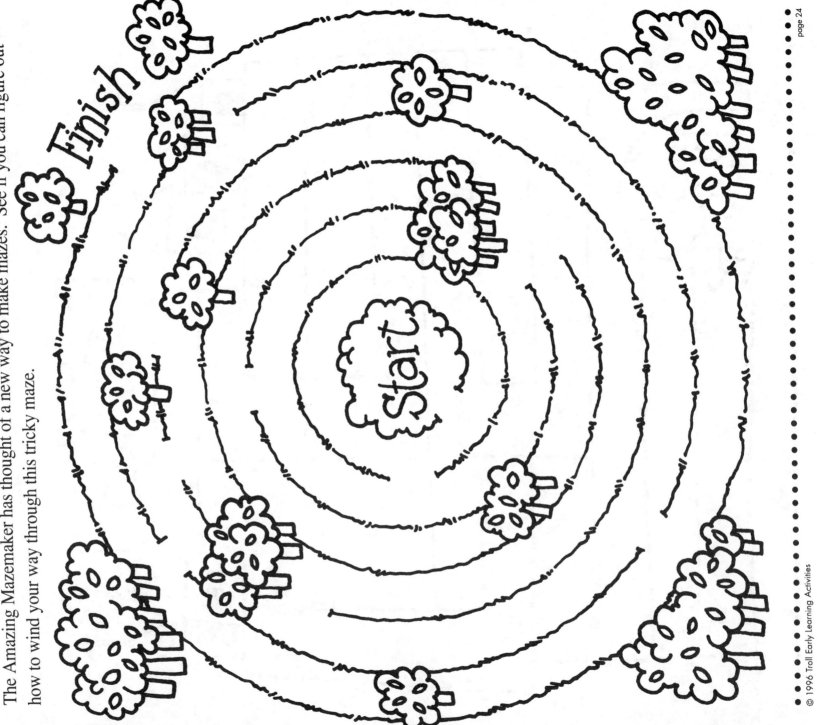

Painting Ideas

1. Marble painting is a very challenging method of painting. You will need a pan, a paper cutout the same size as the bottom of the pan, one or more marbles, and different colors of paint.

2. After each student has chosen a color for the paper bottom, cut the paper to size and lay it at the bottom of the pan. Have the student choose a color or two and place one tablespoon of each color on the paper. Drop a marble into the pan, and, holding the pan with two hands, demonstrate how to maneuver it so the marble rolls into the drops of paint and creates lines over the paper. Encourage students to choose colors that will complement each other.

3. Take the paper out of the pan and let dry. Repeat with each student. Display the paintings on a wall or bulletin board.

4. Sponge painting is a different approach to traditional painting. Precut sponges may be bought at various toy and educational stores. Or use regular square or oval sponges and cut your own shapes.

5. Pour small amounts of paint into different lids (a different color in each one). Assign one sponge to each color and remind students to try to remember which shape belongs to which color.

6. Allow each child to choose the color of paper for his or her painting. Demonstrate how to gently press the sponge into the paint in a lid and then press the sponge to the paper.

7. Encourage students to create their own designs on their papers. Dry the papers and display them on a classroom wall or bulletin board.

8. Other materials useful for painting in a non-traditional fashion include glass scrubbers, cotton swabs, empty glue containers, empty roll-on bottles, blotting containers (such as those used for moistening stamps), anything with a raised surface that would be good for printing, and spray bottles. Good painting surfaces include fingerpaint paper, construction paper, butcher paper, wood scraps, small paper lunch bags, easel paper, thick paper towels, fabric, and cardboard lunch trays.

Nifty Necklaces

Materials:

- different-colored yarn
- scissors
- different-colored straws
- construction paper
- blunt needles
- tape

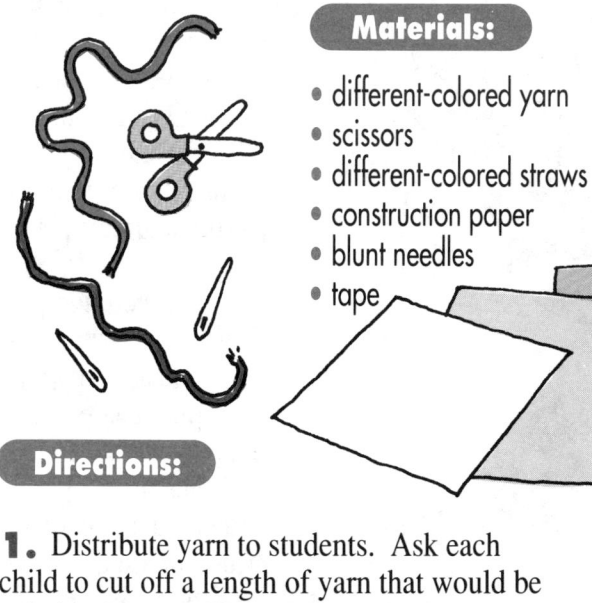

Directions:

1. Distribute yarn to students. Ask each child to cut off a length of yarn that would be suitable for a necklace. The necklaces may be as short or as long as students wish, but they must be able to put it on over their heads. Demonstrate how to knot off one end of the yarn lengths, leaving about 2" excess.

2. Lay out a variety of straws and paper of different colors. Encourage students to cut lengths of straw for their necklaces, but caution them that straw lengths more than 2" will change the shape of their necklaces.

3. Hand out construction paper and ask students to create small geometric shapes with it. They may work with one color or as many as they choose. Have students cut out their designs, roll them into small cylinders, and tape them closed.

4. When all the straw and paper beads are ready, demonstrate to the students how to string them into necklaces. Instruct the children to thread the free end of a length of yarn into the eye of a needle and pull through a "tail" about 4" long.

5. They may begin with either a paper design or a straw. Students push the needle through the center of the paper or inside the straw. Tell students that the straws will stay in place better if paper is added between them; otherwise the straws tend to slip inside each other.

6. When the straws and paper have been added so there is only about 3" left, ask students to take their needles off the yarn length. Knot the two free ends close to the straw or paper.

7. Have a fashion show so that students may show off their creations. Ask each student to write a short paragraph about how he or she made his or her necklace.

8. Collect papers and pick ten students to come up to the front. The rest can be the audience. Choose a student to read the cards; as he or she does so, the student called will walk in front of the audience showing off the necklace. When the first ten are done, call up the next ten, and so on until everyone has had a chance.

Fancy Footwork Games

1. To play "Wiggly Worm," you will need a long jumping rope. Ask students to line up on one side of the rope. Choose two students to hold the ends of the rope. Instruct them to hold it on the floor and begin wiggling it back and forth. Demonstrate for students how they should try to jump over the rope while it is wiggling. If someone touches the rope, he or she is out. Point out to the children that the bigger the wiggles, the more difficult it is to jump over the rope. Continue the game until only one student is left who can jump the wiggling worm.

2. To play "Kick Ball," you will need a large playground ball and chalk. Mark off bases and a pitcher's mound with the chalk as you would for a baseball game. Ask students to line up and count off in ones and twos. All the "ones" will take the field, and all the "twos" will line up to kick. Allow time for the teams to decide who will play which positions and the order of kicking.

3. Have the pitcher roll the ball along the ground directly at the kicker, who stands at home plate. The kicker has three chances to connect with the ball. If the ball is kicked, the player runs to first base and consecutive bases if possible. If the player misses, he or she has made an out. The next kicker comes to kick, and so on until three outs have been made. Then teams switch places. After a prearranged time, such as nine innings, the winner is the team with the most runs scored.

4. To play "'Kick the Can' Obstacle Course," you will need a coffee can with the plastic lid taped on and chalk. Use the chalk to mark out a course on the playground, making a lot of twists and turns along the way. Make it as easy or difficult as the skills of the students permit.

5. Pick a student to go first and set a can in front of him or her on the ground. Tell that player to kick the can along the course to the end. Time each student and let him or her know how long it took to complete the course.

6. After everyone has had a turn, students may try to go again to see if they can decrease their time. Write up a chart showing how practice leads to increased skill, emphasizing the students' decreased course times.

Ball and Cup Game

Materials:

- crayons or markers
- construction paper
- scissors
- plastic cups
- glue
- craft sticks
- transparent tape
- yarn
- large beads

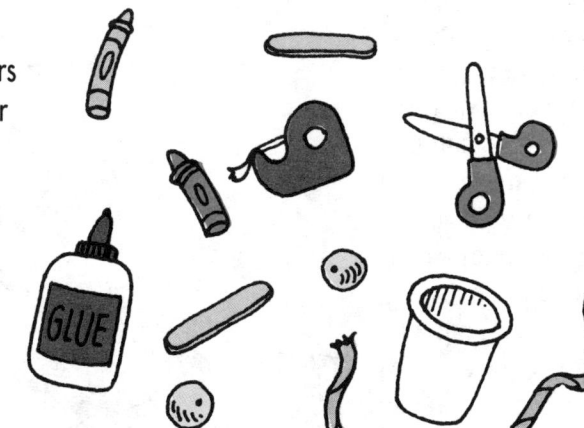

Directions:

1. Cut construction paper to the height and width of a plastic cup. Distribute a piece of paper and crayons or markers to the class and ask them to draw a picture or design. Then show students how to glue their pictures onto a cup. Spread a layer of glue on the back of the picture, then lay the cup at one end of the paper and roll the paper around the cup. Overlap and tape the ends closed.

2. Make a slit at the bottom of the cup and have students stick a craft stick through it, about 1" into the bottom. Help them tape the stick in place, both outside at the bottom of the cup and inside the cup if possible.

3. At the inside base of each cup, tie a 12" length of yarn around the stick. Tape in place. Slip a bead through the other end of the yarn and knot it so the bead cannot slip off.

4. To play, have students hold the stick with the ball hanging down. The children should move the stick in a forward arc position so the ball will begin swinging forward and up. The bigger the movements, the bigger the swing. Students may move the cup as the bead swings in order to catch it in the cup. See how many times in a row they can catch the balls.

Paddleball

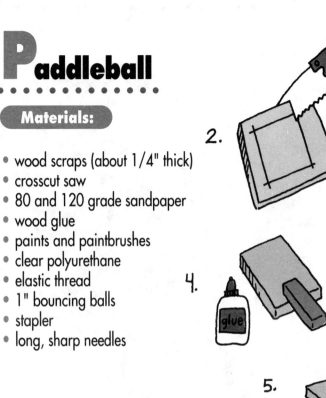

Materials:

- wood scraps (about 1/4" thick)
- crosscut saw
- 80 and 120 grade sandpaper
- wood glue
- paints and paintbrushes
- clear polyurethane
- elastic thread
- 1" bouncing balls
- stapler
- long, sharp needles

Directions:

1. This activity is best done with just one or two students at a time under close supervision. Try to find a woodworking table, which many kindergarten classes have. Or you may use a clamp and a table.

2. Give the first students wood scraps and have them measure a 5" x 5" paddle piece and a 5" x 2" handle. To begin the sawing, help the student make three or four backward cuts. That is, hold the saw and bring it toward you at a 45° angle to the wood.

3. Try making a forward cut; if the saw goes through, continue in a forward and backward motion. If not, try some more backward cuts. When the wood has been cut to size, call the next student to come measure and cut. The first student should begin sanding down the rough edges of his or her wood pieces using 80 grade sandpaper. When the edges have been smoothed, he or she should switch to 120 grade sandpaper.

4. When the paddle and handle have been smoothed, overlap the two by about 1" and glue the handle to the paddle. Hold in place for a few minutes before leaving to dry. Give students paints and paintbrushes to decorate the paddles and handles. When the paint is dry, brush a thin coat of clear polyurethane over the paddle to help keep the paint from flaking off and to protect the wood.

5. Help students make a knot at one end of a 15" length of elastic thread. Staple this end to the center of the paddle. Then help students thread the other end of the thread through the eye of a long needle and stick the needle through a small bounceable ball. Knot the end so it will not go back through the ball.

6. To play, students hold the paddle by the handle and bounce the ball against the paddle section. See how many times in a row they can bounce the ball off the paddle.

Keep Your Eye on the Ball!

1. Gather a group of students around a small table. Place three plastic cups upside down on the table in a row. Make sure the cups are not transparent.
2. Show the students a ball small enough to fit in the cups. Place the ball under one inverted cup and switch the cup with another one while students watch. Ask them under which cup the ball can be found. Show students whether the ball is under the cup they chose. If not, show them which cup is hiding the ball.
3. Take the ball from under the cup and try it again. This time, move the two cups a little faster. Decrease the switching time until students can find the ball easily. Then change the method—switch all three cups around. Do this until students can find the ball, and then move the cups a little faster.
4. When students become familiar with the game, allow them to try being the person who switches the cups. For added fun, use two balls and four cups.

Microart

- 5" x 20" oaktag strips
- scissors
- clear plastic wrap
- transparent tape
- straws
- collage materials
- tweezers
- glue

Directions:

1. Give each student a strip of oaktag. Demonstrate how to make folds in the oaktag at 5" intervals, making sure all folds face the same way.

2. On one of the 5" sides, help students cut out a circle with a 4" diameter. Cut a 5" x 5" square from clear plastic wrap and glue to the underside of the cutout side. Then tape the two end sides together to form a box. Make sure the "magnifying glass" side is facing up.

3. Distribute collage materials and inform students that they will be making a picture under the magnifying glass. However, the only way they can place the materials for their picture is by using tweezers.

4. Spread glue on the oaktag side opposite the magnifying glass and then place materials on it. Or spread glue on the materials and then place the materials on the oaktag opposite the magnifying glass using the tweezers. Remind students that their pictures should be miniature because they are under a magnifying glass.

5. Arrange the art in a display for students to browse through during free time. Cut a magnifying glass shape from paper and entitle the display "Microart."

The Locked Door

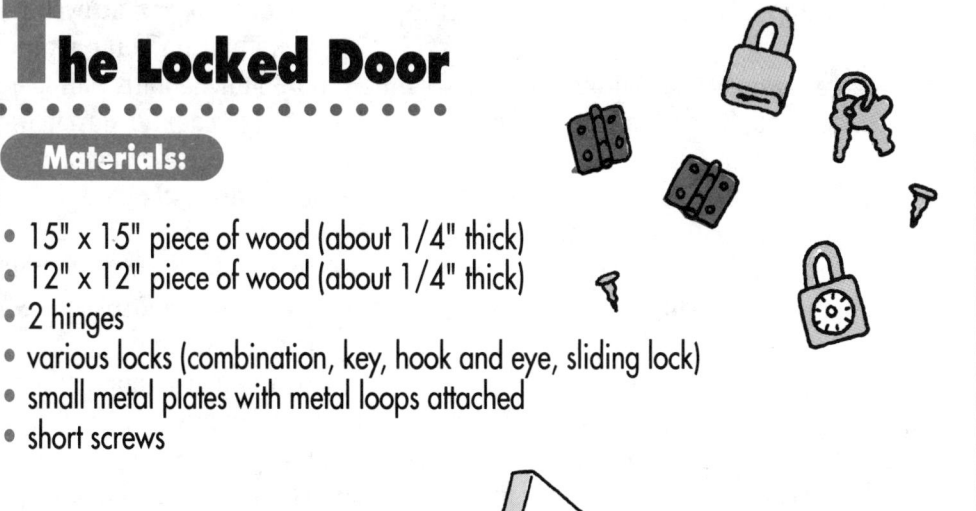

- 15" x 15" piece of wood (about 1/4" thick)
- 12" x 12" piece of wood (about 1/4" thick)
- 2 hinges
- various locks (combination, key, hook and eye, sliding lock)
- small metal plates with metal loops attached
- short screws

3. Follow directions for attaching a hook and eye lock and a sliding lock onto the door and frame. For the combination and key locks, you must first place the metal plates with loops attached onto the door and frame, level with each other. Then attach the combination lock onto one looped plate pair, and the key lock onto the other looped plate pair.

4. Give the students the combination and the key for the locks and ask them to try to open the door after they have read the riddle and think they know the answer.

5. For added challenge, make all the locks combination locks or key locks. Students will have to work out the right combinations or fit the right keys in the locks before they will open.

Directions:

1. Lay a 15" x 15" board down on a flat surface. Place a 12" x 12" board on top, centering it. Follow directions on a hinge package to secure the smaller board to the larger one using two hinges. This will be the door.

2. Under the door, tape a picture. On the door, write a riddle about the picture for which students can check their answers only if they open the door.

All Tied Up

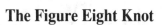

Challenge students to learn how to tie some or all of the knots described below. Reproduce the knot pictures on page 34 once for each child. Work through each knot once or twice as a class. Then encourage students to pair up and time each other as they try to tie these knots.

The Figure Eight Knot

1. Fold the rope in half and cross the right end over the middle of the rope on the left side.

2. Holding the end that is now on the left side, loop it under the rope now on the right side, forming a figure eight.

3. Take the same end and cross it over the top circle of the figure eight straight up to the top of it, pushing it under the loop. Pull tight.

The Eye Knot

1. Fold the rope in half and hold the two strands together.

2. Form a simple knot, leaving the loop at the top. The loop may be made into any size at this point. Pull tight.

The Slip Knot

1. Make a loop in the left end of the rope by crossing the left end under the rope then over the rope.

2. Thread the left end through the loop and pull through.

3. Holding the loop, pull on the left strand to tighten the knot. The right strand may be used to make the loop smaller or larger. To undo the knot, pull on the right end while holding the left end still.

The Square Knot

1. For this knot, you will need two ropes. Find the middle of one rope and form a loop.

2. Put one end of the other rope over and under the right side of the loop.

3. Take that same end and lay it over the first rope. Thread the end over and under the left side of the loop. Even out the ropes so the knot is at the center of both.

4. Holding both ends of both ropes, pull tightly. This knot is used for joining two ropes and can easily be undone when the ends are pushed toward each other, loosening the knot.

Name _____

All Tied Up

1. The Figure Eight Knot

2. The Eye Knot

3. The Slip Knot

4. The Square Knot

Timed Skill Tests

1. Timed tests are a wonderful way to help students practice small motor skills. Set aside a predesignated period of time for each session (e.g., one, two, or three minutes) for the timed test. Repeat each type of test for a week or for as long it takes for students to master the task.

2. Begin by asking each student to write his or her name on a piece of paper. Then set a timer and ask each student to write his or her name as many times as possible (and as neatly as possible!) until the timer goes off.

3. Ask each student to count how many times he or she has written the name and record the number at the top of the piece of paper.

4. Repeat the exercise the next day. Ask students to see if they have improved. Have volunteers tell how many times they wrote their names the second day.

5. Continue for several more days. Reinforce to students that it is not important how many times they write their names, but rather that they improve their totals.

6. Repeat with other small motor tasks, such as buttoning, tying shoes, snapping fingers, and coloring shapes.

Weaving Patterns

- 7" x 7" oaktag squares of different colors
- scissors
- different-colored yarn

1.

2.

3.

4.

1. Distribute squares of oaktag to each student. Demonstrate how to cut slits on opposite sides, about 1/4" apart and 1/2" into the oaktag.

2. Using long lengths of yarn, show students how to knot one end, then begin looping it onto the slits of the oaktag square, starting with the first slit on one side, crossing over to the first slit on the opposite side, then moving back across to the second slit on the original side, and so on. When finished, the oaktag should be covered by lines of yarn. If students wish, they may cut off their length of yarn and tie on a new color. Remind students to be sure their knots are tight.

3. Next, show the students how to weave an 8" length of yarn through the lines of yarn on the board: over the first line, under the second, over the third, under the fourth, and so on until the last line. Continue with another 8" length of yarn, alternating the pattern. Students may use one or two colors, or as many as they choose. When the board is filled, yarn lengths may be trimmed to the size of the board or left to hang a bit off.

4. Cut a 5" length of yarn and slip it into one of the yarn loops on the oaktag. Knot the ends. This will be a loop for hanging the weaving design. If students wish to create more weavings, encourage them to make different designs. For example, a child may wish to weave two strands of one color, then three strands of another, repeating the process until the end of the board.

Design Booklets

Directions:

• two 9" x 12" sheets of white paper
• dark marker
• hole puncher
• four 9" x 12" pieces of oaktag
• ring binders

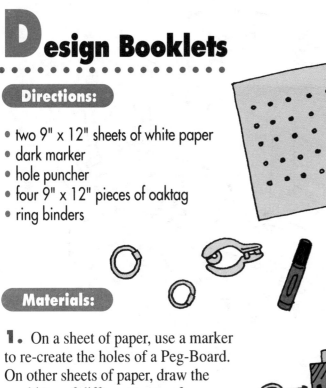

Materials:

1. On a sheet of paper, use a marker to re-create the holes of a Peg-Board. On other sheets of paper, draw the markings of different types of geoboards (for example, circle geoboards or square geoboards). Reproduce these sheets several times.

2. Gather all the Peg-Board sheets and punch three holes down the left side of the stack. For a cover, take two pieces of oaktag and punch three holes in the same position as the holes punched in the Peg-Board sheets. Bind covers and Peg-Board sheets together with a three-ring binder. Ask a volunteer to design a cover for the Peg-Board booklet. Repeat the process for the geoboard booklet.

3. Show the booklets to the class. Explain that the booklets are for storing their Peg-Board and geoboard designs. When a student creates a design on either board, he or she may copy it into the correct booklet. Other students may then copy the designs when they use the boards. They may also elaborate on designs they find in the booklets and then copy their own new designs into the booklets.

4. As pages in the booklets are used up, add more sheets of paper with the correct markings on them. Booklets can be stored in the math center along with the boards, pegs, and rubber bands.

Graham Cracker House

Materials:

- 5" x 5" squares of cardboard
- graham crackers
- peanut butter
- paper plates
- plastic knives
- mini marshmallows
- small candies
- colored cellophane
- ribbon

Directions:

1. Explain to the students that they will be making a graham cracker house on a cardboard base. Give each student a cardboard square and some graham crackers. Scoop peanut butter onto plates and place a plate at each workstation. Distribute plastic knives to the students.

2. Show students how to stand a cracker upright and stick it to the cardboard square by adding peanut butter to the base of the cracker. Add another wall at a 45° angle to the first, sticking it to the floor as well as to the first wall. Continue adding walls until a square is formed. Make a roof by spreading peanut butter on the tops of the walls and placing two crackers on top at a 45° angle.

3. Next, students may decorate their houses with marshmallows and small candies. They may stick the small objects onto the house using the peanut butter. A peanut butter walkway up to the house can be formed from peanut butter and mini marshmallows. Trees may be made by stacking marshmallows on top of each other and using candies for leaves (all stuck together with peanut butter).

4. When students have completed their houses, display them. Encourage students to share how they put together their houses and explain the special touches. If desired, wrap the houses in colored cellophane and tie closed with a ribbon. Students may bring their houses home as special gifts.

Alphabet Autobiographies

D, my name is Dan...

1. Gather the class together and have the children sit cross-legged in a circle. Inform them that they will be playing a game to the beat of "Lap, Clap, Snap, Snap." Try it with the class before beginning the game and practice for a few minutes so all will be comfortable with the beat.

2. Explain to the class that they will be chanting as they keep the beat. The chant is about a made-up spouse, where they live, and what they sell for a living. As each player goes, he or she must begin each name with the next letter of the alphabet. Do the first verse yourself, saying, for example, "A my name is Ana and my husband's name is Al; we come from Alaska and we sell apples." The chant begins on the lap beat. (Boys will substitute the word *wife* for *husband*.) The next player would begin with "B my name is . . ." and continue substituting names in the chant that begin with the letter *B*. Each consecutive player will use the next letter in the alphabet.

3. If a player does not keep the beat during his or her turn, he or she is out. If a player uses the wrong letter of the alphabet, he or she is out. The last player left in the game is the winner.

Name _____

Follow the boxed color key to color in the picture below. A funny picture will be revealed.

COLOR KEY	
1/2 blue	1/3 green
1/4 red	1/5 yellow

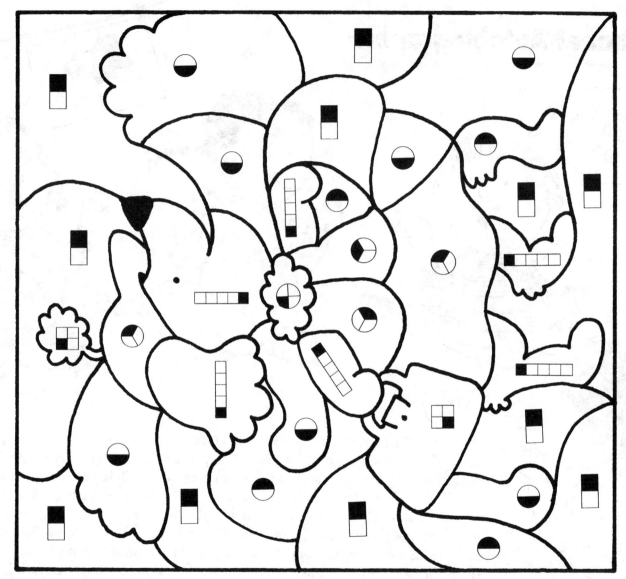

Marble in the Middle

1. Gather a small group of students in a circle and ask them to sit. Give each student five marbles and place one in the center of the circle. Around the marble, draw a chalk circle on the floor about 5" in diameter.

2. Choose one student to go first. From his or her place in the circle, this player will roll his or her marble towards the marble in the center, trying to knock it out of the center circle.

3. If the first player misses the marble, the marbles are left in place and the next player goes. If a player hits the middle marble out of its circle either with his or her marble or by striking another marble that then strikes the middle marble, he or she collects the middle marble as well as all the marbles that are on the playing surface. The middle marble must be hit in order to collect any other marbles. A new marble must be placed in the center circle after a winning turn.

4. A player who loses all his or her marbles is out of the game. The player who captures all the marbles is the winner.

tring Configurations

1. Choose a partner with whom to demonstrate the game to the other students. You will need a 24" length of string to play. Knot the ends together and wrap the string loop once around each of your hands. Raise your hands up, palms facing each other. Slip the middle finger of your right hand under the loop around the left hand and bring the string back toward your right hand. Slip the middle finger of your left hand under the loop around your right hand and bring the string back toward your left hand, making a string "boat."

2. Your partner can then place the pointer finger and thumb of each hand in the triangles formed on the sides of the string boat. He or she will pinch together those fingers and bring the string triangles over the tops of the string along the sides of the boat, and continue bringing his or her hands apart until the string is taut.

3. The first player should then use both hands to try to grab the string looped around those fingers and create a new shape. Continue making new shapes until the string either loses its shape or becomes too tight. Encourage students to create new and challenging configurations and share them with their classmates.

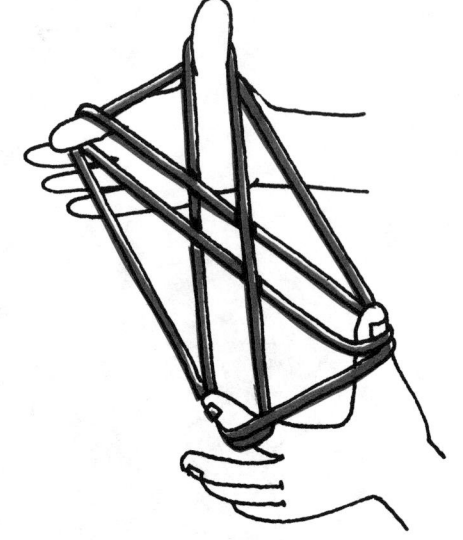

Catch It If You Can

1. Divide the class into two teams and ask the teams to line up facing each other, about 2' apart. Players opposite one another will be partners.

2. Give all the students on one line a small object, such as a bean bag. On the word *Throw*, have these students toss their objects to their partners. If anyone drops the object, he or she and the partner both are out. If the partner catches the object, both players are still in the game.

3. Have those partners still in the game move 1' farther away from each other. On the word *Throw*, the players throw the object back to their partners. Again, if anyone drops the object, he or she and the partner are out. If a partner catches the object, both partners stay in the game and move another foot farther away.

4. The game continues this way until there is only one pair of partners left.

Clothespin Match

Materials:

- cardboard circles, 9" in diameter
- markers
- clothespins, the type that open and close
- blank stickers

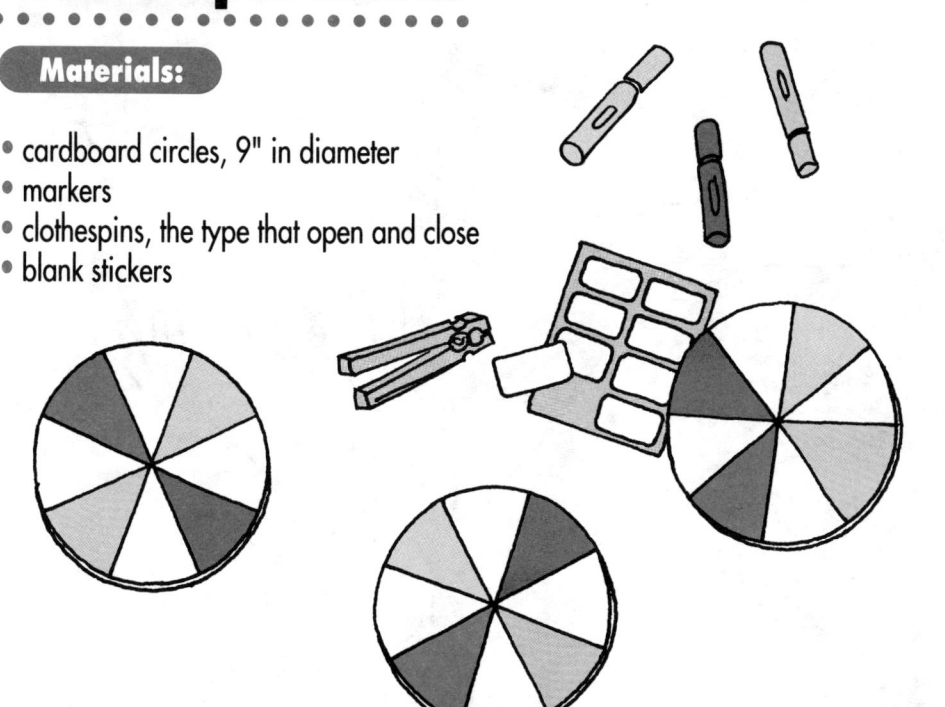

Directions:

1. Create a color-matching game for younger students. Begin by dividing a 9" cardboard circle into eight wedges. Color each wedge a different color.

2. Using blank stickers, write a matching color name on each sticker. Then place the appropriate sticker onto its clothespin.

3. To play, ask students to read the names on the clothespins and then attach the clothespins to the wedges with the matching colors.

4. Another game for young students is a counting game. Divide a 9" cardboard circle into eight wedges and draw a picture of objects numbering zero to seven in each wedge. (The numbers may range as high as the skill of the students and need not be in consecutive order.) On blank stickers, write numerals that match the number of objects in each wedge on the circle. Then stick the labels on clothespins.

5. To play, have students count how many objects are in each wedge and then attach the clothespins to the appropriate wedges.

6. A prereading activity for younger students will help them learn to recognize their own names as well as their friends' names. Divide as many 9" cardboard circles into four wedges as necessary to have one wedge for each child in the class.

7. Glue a photograph of each student into a wedge. Write the students' names on stickers and place them on clothespins. To play, students will match the names to the photographs.

8. For older students, games may be played matching words that make compound words (for example, you may write *cup* on a wedge and *cake* on a clothespin), math equations with their answers, parts of a plant with their names, objects with the rooms they belong in, and a sequence of events with the number order in which the sequence occurs.

Name _____

W indy Day Mix-Up

Use crayons of different colors to trace a line from each person flying a kite to the kite he or she is flying. Then color the picture.

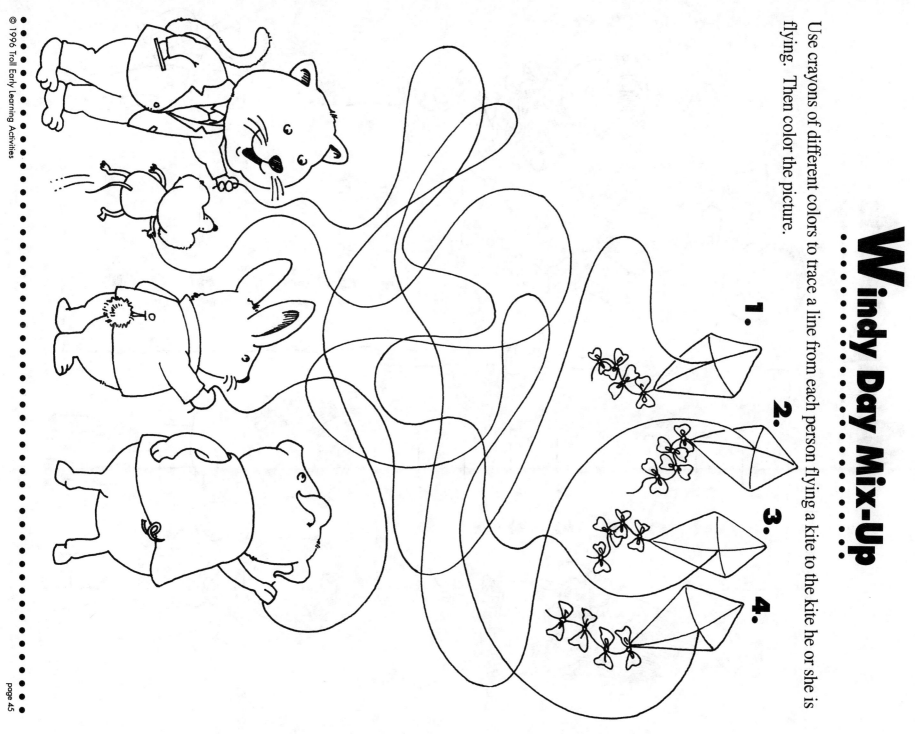

1.

2.

3.

4.

Name _____

Missing Letters

Fill in the missing letters below.

1. r __ t
2. d __ f
3. h __ j
4. p __ r
5. w __ y
6. b __ d
7. l __ n
8. x __ z

9. o __ q
10. k __ m
11. __ d __
12. __ r __
13. __ b __
14. __ t __
15. __ o __

Name _____

Pattern Pictures
. . . .

Look at each of the blocks below. Color the boxes according to the color written on each one.
Color in the blocks below each pattern following the same color pattern.

1.

red	blue	red	blue

2.

green	yellow	red	green	yellow	red

3.

black	orange	orange	black	orange	orange

4.

purple	white	purple	purple	white	purple

5.

red	red	red	yellow

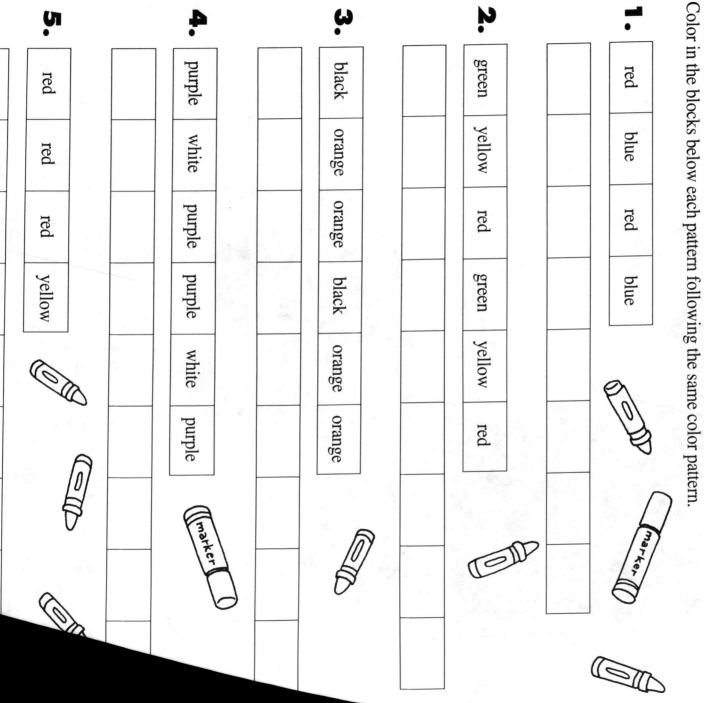

page 47

w...
cut ...

2. H... ...ndomly
draw a... ...pots (from zero
to six) on... ...ladybug. Tell the class
to make sure that the ladybugs in
each column have different numbers
of spots.

3. Explain to the children that the
class will be playing bingo using the
ladybug game cards. Call out a random number (from zero to six) paired
with one of the letters in the word
bugs. For example, you might call
out "G2." If a student has a ladybug
with two circles on it in his or her *G*
column, that player should color in
both circles with a crayon or marker.

4. Keep a record of the numbers that
are called on the chalkboard. When a
student has colored in all the ladybugs
in a horizontal or vertical row, he or
she should call out "Bingo!"

5. For variation, have students complete a letter *X*, a picture frame (the
perimeter of the bingo board), or the
entire board before calling out
"Bingo!"

Ladybug Bingo

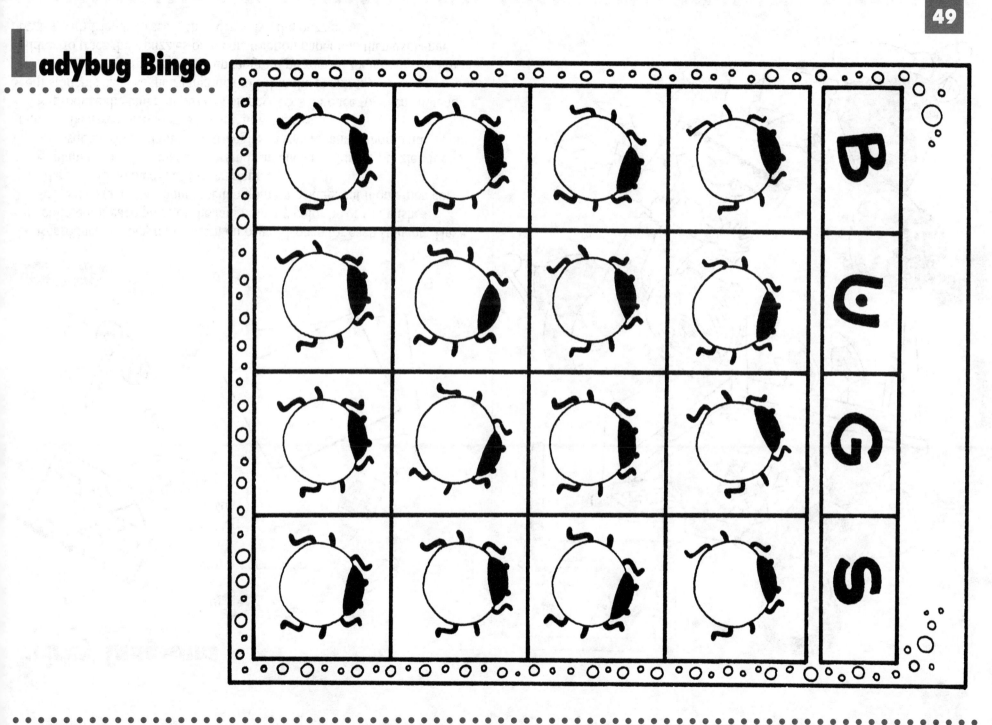

Tricky Tangrams

© 1996 Troll Early Learning Activities

Materials:

- crayons or markers
- glue
- oaktag
- scissors

Directions:

1. Reproduce the tangram pattern on page 51 once for each student. Have each child color each piece of the tangram any color he or she wishes.

2. Ask each student to mount the tangram on oaktag, cut it out, then cut apart the individual pieces of the tangram.

3. Explain to the class that a tangram is an ancient Chinese puzzle. It consists of a square divided into five triangles, a square, and a rhomboid. A tangram can be assembled to make many new figures.

4. Reproduce the tangram puzzles on pages 52–53 once for each student. See if students can use their tangrams to fill in the puzzles.

5. Allow students time to make up tangram puzzles of their own. Tell the children to trace their puzzles onto construction paper and then exchange puzzles with friends to see if they can solve the puzzles.

Name _____

Pattern Pictures
· · · · · · · · · · · · · · · · · ·

Look at each of the blocks below. Color the boxes according to the color written on each one.

Color in the blocks below each pattern following the same color pattern.

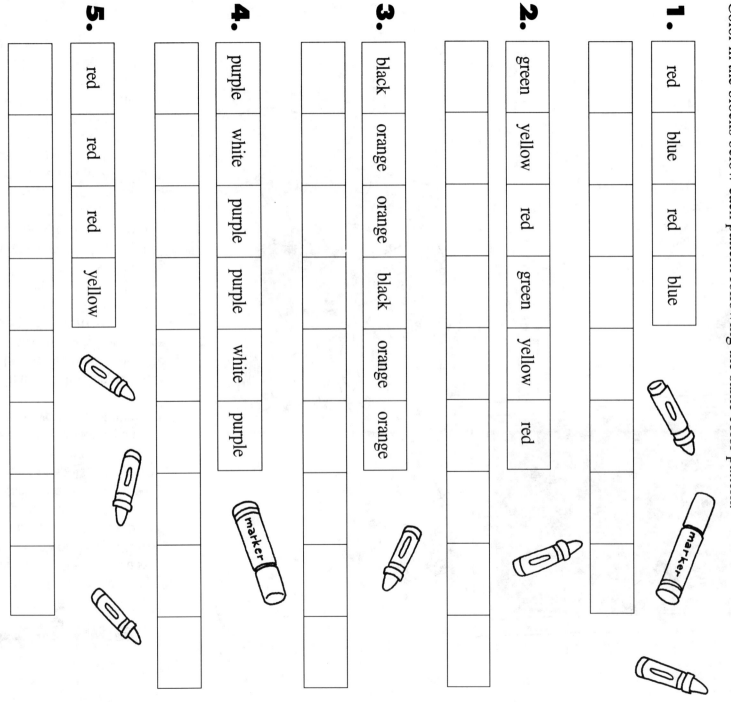

1. | red | blue | red | blue | | | | |

2. | green | yellow | red | green | yellow | red | | |

3. | black | orange | orange | black | orange | orange | | |

4. | purple | white | purple | purple | white | purple | | |

5. | red | red | yellow | | | | | |

adybug Bingo

1. Reproduce the game card on page 49 once for each child in the class. Tell students to color the borders, write their names across the top, and cut out the game cards.

2. Have each student randomly draw a number of spots (from zero to six) on each ladybug. Tell the class to make sure that the ladybugs in each column have different numbers of spots.

3. Explain to the children that the class will be playing bingo using the ladybug game cards. Call out a random number (from zero to six) paired with one of the letters in the word *bugs*. For example, you might call out "G2." If a student has a ladybug with two circles on it in his or her *G* column, that player should color in both circles with a crayon or marker.

4. Keep a record of the numbers that are called on the chalkboard. When a student has colored in all the ladybugs in a horizontal or vertical row, he or she should call out "Bingo!"

5. For variation, have students complete a letter *X*, a picture frame (the perimeter of the bingo board), or the entire board before calling out "Bingo!"

Ladybug Bingo

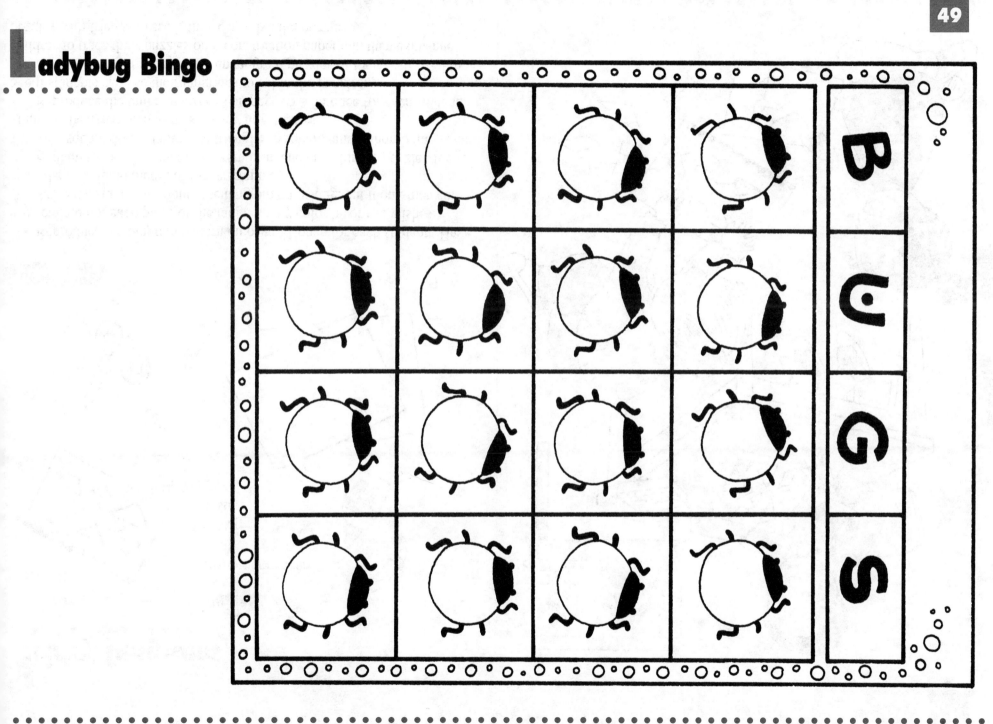

Tricky Tangrams

Materials:

- crayons or markers
- glue
- oaktag
- scissors

Directions:

1. Reproduce the tangram pattern on page 51 once for each student. Have each child color each piece of the tangram any color he or she wishes.

2. Ask each student to mount the tangram on oaktag, cut it out, then cut apart the individual pieces of the tangram.

3. Explain to the class that a tangram is an ancient Chinese puzzle. It consists of a square divided into five triangles, a square, and a rhomboid. A tangram can be assembled to make many new figures.

4. Reproduce the tangram puzzles on pages 52–53 once for each student. See if students can use their tangrams to fill in the puzzles.

5. Allow students time to make up tangram puzzles of their own. Tell the children to trace their puzzles onto construction paper and then exchange puzzles with friends to see if they can solve the puzzles.

Tricky Tangrams

Tricky Tangrams

Name _____

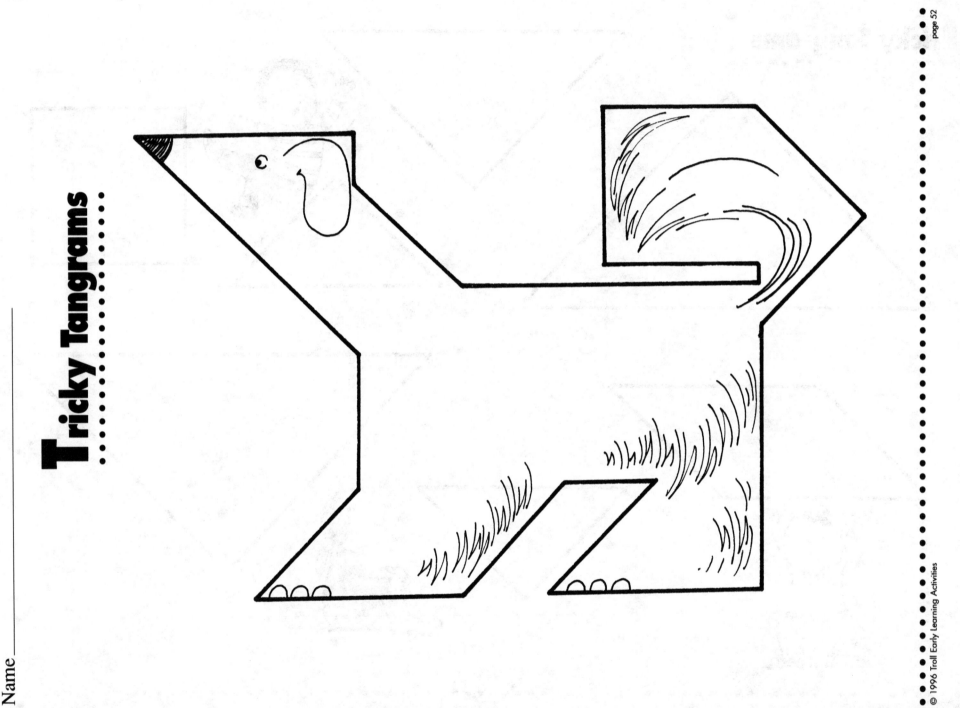

Tricky Tangrams

What's Missing?

Complete the drawings in the right column so that they match the drawings in the left column.

Paper Planes

2.

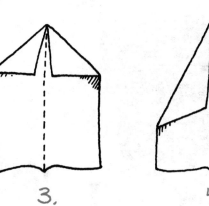

3.

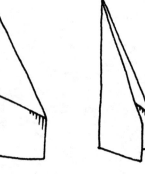

4.

5.

6.

7.

Directions:

1. Distribute a sheet of 9" x 12" construction paper or 8 1/2" x 11" photocopy paper to each student.

2. Have each student fold the paper in half lengthwise.

3. Tell students to fold the upper left and right corners down into right triangles, as shown.

4. Have each child repeat the step, folding the upper corners in toward the center line.

5. Next, fold the entire plane in half, as shown.

6. Fold down a flap on each side of the plane to make wings, as shown.

7. Bring the wings up so that they are at right angles to the center of the plane. Hold the plane in the center to fly it.

8. Encourage students to have contests to see whose plane flies the farthest, the fastest, or the highest. If desired, provide students with more paper so that they may experiment with new plane designs.

Halloween Stencils

Materials:

- glue
- oaktag
- scissors
- single-edged razor blade or artist's knife
- stenciling materials

Directions:

1. Stencils are a fun and interesting way to help students practice their small motor control. Reproduce the holiday stencils on pages 57–58 twice. Mount the stencils on oaktag and cut away excess oaktag, leaving an ample margin between the mounted stencils and the outer edges.

2. Use a razor blade or sharp artist's knife to cut out the stencil interiors.

3. Place the stencils in the art center for students to use to make Halloween projects. Suggested projects include Halloween cards, murals, storybooks, and games. Provide students with construction paper, poster paper, file folders, crayons and markers, paints, and other materials as necessary.

Halloween Stencils

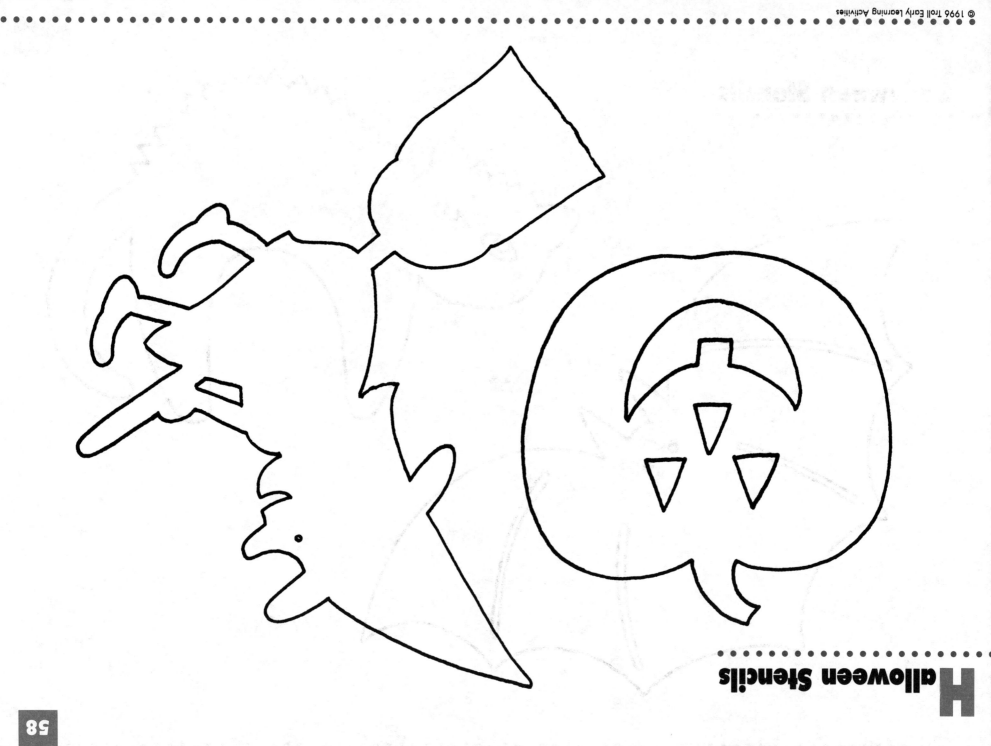

Dandy Dreidels

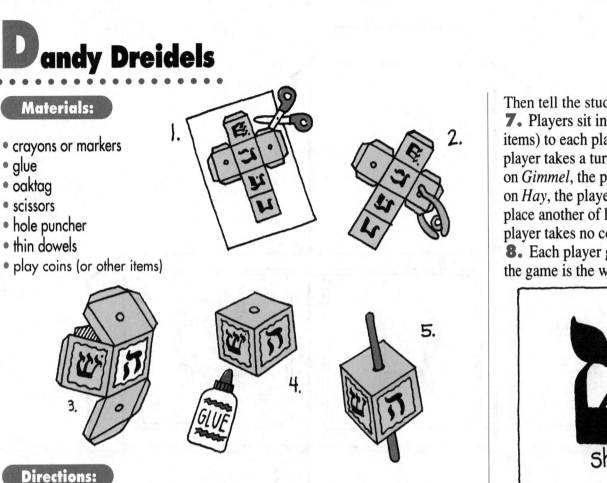

Materials:

- crayons or markers
- glue
- oaktag
- scissors
- hole puncher
- thin dowels
- play coins (or other items)

Directions:

1. For winter holiday fun, reproduce the dreidel pattern on page 60 once for each child. Have students color the dreidels, mount them on oaktag, and cut them out.
2. On each dreidel pattern, punch two small holes where indicated.
3. Have each child fold the dreidel pattern along the lines and then fold the dreidel into a cube shape, as shown.
4. Help each student glue the dreidel together along the flaps.
5. Place a dowel through the holes, as shown. Make sure the dowel fits snugly.
6. Explain to the class what each symbol means (see box at right).

Then tell the students that they are going to play a game with a dreidel.
7. Players sit in a circle. Begin by distributing ten play coins (or other items) to each player. Have each player place a coin in the center. The first player takes a turn spinning a dreidel. If a player spins and the dreidel lands on *Gimmel*, the player takes all the coins in the center. If the dreidel lands on *Hay*, the player takes half the coins. If it lands on *Shin*, the player must place another of his or her coins in the center. And if it lands on *Nun*, the player takes no coins.
8. Each player gets five turns. The player with the most coins at the end of the game is the winner.

shin

hay

gimmel

nun

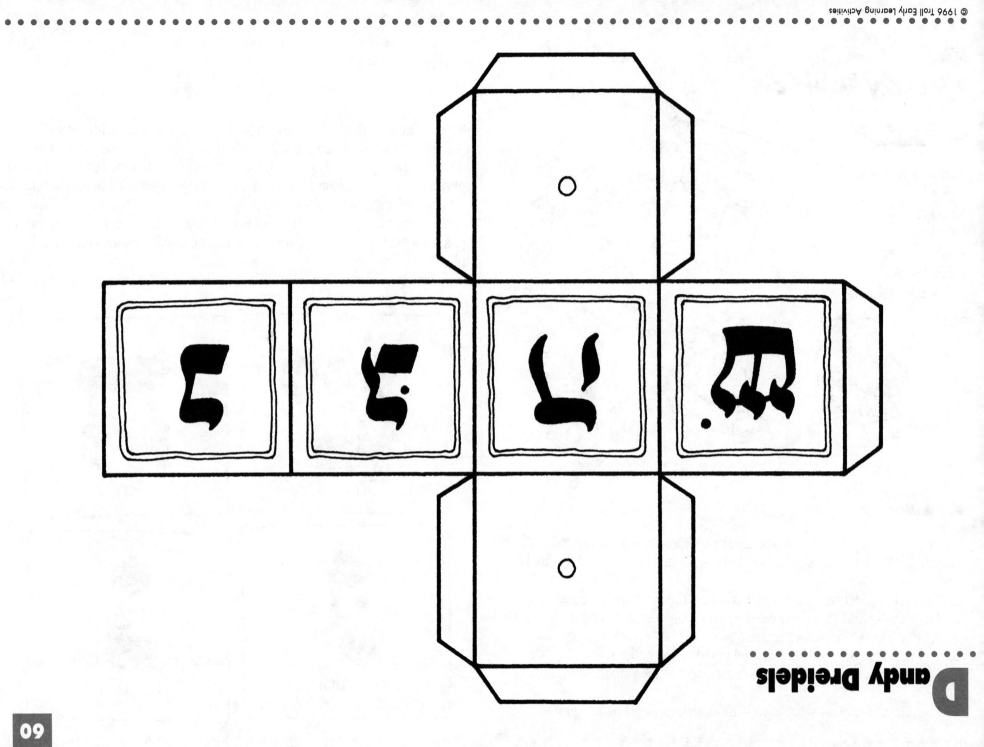

Miniflag Fun

1.

2.

3.

4.

Directions:

1. Distribute a piece of 8 1/2" x 11" photocopy paper to each student. Have students hold the papers vertically in front of them.

2. Tell each student to cut a vertical line approximately 3" away from the left edge of the paper. Have them extend the line approximately 7" from the lower edge of the paper.

3. Show students how to fold the part of the paper to the right of the line in half, toward the back and top of the paper. Then fold the paper again, from the back toward the front so that the fold line of the paper on the right is flush with the top of the cut line. Tape in place to hold.

4. To make the flagpole, roll the paper on the left into a tight circle. Tape in place to hold.

5. Give the children crayons and markers to use to decorate their flags. Encourage students to draw something on their flags that shows their personalities, interests, families, or other important things about themselves.

6. Display the flags on a bulletin board titled "Our Own Grand Old Flags."

abc

abc

Presented to:

... for superior handwriting skills...

Teacher _____ Date _____

Award

Presented To

For Super-duper Dexterity

teacher _____ date _____

Answers

page 11

1. T	4. Y
2. F	5. Z
3. K	

Answers for the second part of this exercise will vary.

page 23

page 24

page 40

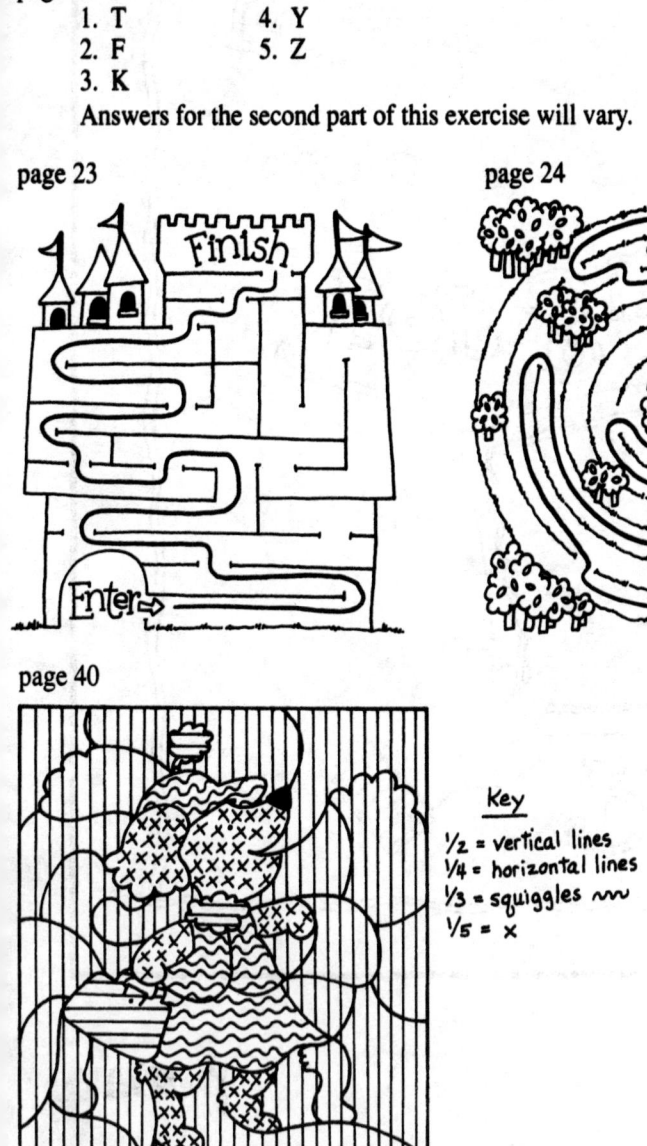

Key

½ = vertical lines
¼ = horizontal lines
⅓ = squiggles ∼∼
⅕ = x

page 45

kite 1—bunny
kite 2—pig
kite 3—cat
kite 4—mouse

page 46

1. r<u>s</u>t	9. o<u>p</u>q
2. d<u>e</u>f	10. k<u>l</u>m
3. hi<u>j</u>	11. <u>c</u>de
4. p<u>q</u>r	12. <u>q</u>rs
5. wx<u>y</u>	13. ab<u>c</u>
6. b<u>c</u>d	14. <u>s</u>tu
7. l<u>m</u>n	15. <u>n</u>op
8. x<u>y</u>z	

page 54